Lonely Musings

Lonely Musings

Paul Hubbard

ISBN 978-0-578-00070-1

Contents

Family: Where I'm From, Where I'm Going

Broken Circle

Why me? Why you?
  Why must I suffer?
  Why must you feel such pain?
A touch. A simple touch.
  That's all I've wanted from you.
  Why were you slain?
Morning. Noon. Night.
  I always think about you
  And the relationship we never had.
My family. My friends.
  They see my face and my manner.
  They all say I resemble you, Dad.
A thought. Just a thought.
  To see each other once in this life;
  Is that too much to ask?
Yeah, I guess so.
  But to change the past and have met you,
  I'd accomplish any task.
Oh Lord. Oh God.
  Where did I come from?
  Where did my Father go?
Back before, before my birth,
  Did we ever meet?
  Did we each other know?
My breath of life,
  The first air You breathed into my lungs-
  Was it his last saved by You for me?
If so,
  Please tell me, Lord,
  That I'm his living memory.

My heart.
  A sea of confusion,
  That never seems to cease.
I always think of you
  And miss you.
  My hurt will never ease.
Wherever you are,
  Are your heart and mind hindered?
  Does your sorrow ail you like mine?
I don't cry;
  Out loud at least.
  But at times (inside) I silently whimper and whine.
My sleep
  At night is broken, restless.
  My dreams lack peace and quiet.
I awake,
  No recollection of my dreams.
  But I feel as though I've lived through a riot.
Are you lonely?
  Do you long for my touch?
  I need and want yours, too.
I never met you,
  But do you think you can believe
  That I miss and truly love you?

We never touched, never met,
  Never even saw each other.
But I love you, Dad, nonetheless;
  And I know you'll be with me forever.

Sunflower

Grandma.
I miss you.
I still love you.
My sunflower.

You make me think of warm summer days,
The sun soaking us in its life-giving rays.
Grandma's house is where we always wanted to go;
Not the park, or the pool, or the motion picture show.
Grandma's house; where we could run and play and
     laugh!
Ah yeah, the fun we had. You don't know the half.
Grandma was always there for us,
Her children: adopted and real.
One time, she fed a woman on a bus,
Gave a stranger her last meal.
Why, you may ask, would she do such a deed?
It's easy: Someday, one of hers may be a stranger in
     need.
Grandma was like that, always putting her children
     first,
For us, I know she'd go hungry; I'm sure she'd endure
     thirst.
My Grandma is special, as all grandmas are;
But now she's in Heaven, the firmament's brightest star.
I miss you, Grandma; I can't stress it enough.
When you were here with us, life seemed a little less
     rough.
You touched us all, Grandma –
Our hearts, minds, and souls.
Protector and caregiver
Were only two of your roles.

You were a teacher, who taught us,
Among other things,
That this world isn't fair
And birds don't always sing.
You taught us to love
And do many kind deeds.
That acts of kindness
Multiply like weeds.
To us all you're a saint
And a true inspiration.
You deserve our respect and love,
Honor and admiration.
You made me a better man
And this world a better place.
Your life was a benefit
To the entire human race.

I love you, Grandma.
I truly appreciate the time you spent here with us.

Circle Completed

A new little life.
A new star in the sky.
Another beginning.
Tears of joy from my eyes.
Today a child was born,
But not just any child.
I saw my son's birth,
The birth of a man-child.
His eyes trust me
To treat him right.
With my voice and a touch,
I subdue his fright.
His very life brings me joy,
Like none I've ever known.
And as long as he breathes,
I'll never be alone.
I've been alone, in a sense,
From my very first day.
For before I was born,
My Father passed away.
I've seen and touched my new son,
Now all is well with my soul.
I want for nothing more;
I need not even grow old.
I completed a circle,
That wasn't really started.
Because of this broken circle,
I grew up broken-hearted.
But I rejoice in the fact,
That my son won't know this feeling.
This is a deep-seated agony,
That sometimes sends me reeling.

But I must honor yesterday,
By looking to tomorrow.
I must dwell on my happiness,
And lay to rest my sorrow.
I must focus on my son,
And the times I have yet to see.
I must send him charging forth,
To be what he's meant to be.
I must teach him to fly
And prepare him to soar.
I must give him the keys
To open every door.

I love and miss my Father;
I cherish and love my son.
I was given a broken circle at birth,
But now my circle's done.

A Father's Prayer

As I lay me down to sleep,
I pray your dreams are kind and sweet.
Dreams of those you know and love,
And of those who watch you from above.
As I tuck you in to rest,
I know I must be at my best.
I must teach you everything I know,
Give you my wisdom as you grow.
As I turn your night light on,
I wish your daily tensions gone.
Each day you have to learn so much,
All about the world and such.
As I feed you spoon by spoon,
I know you'll feed yourself real soon.
You'll do more and more each day,
As you interact and play.
As you hold my leg to walk,
I listen as you start to talk.
I can't quite understand you yet,
But the meaning of your words I get.
I love you more each day, my Son;
We both grow much and still have fun.
But, one day you'll become a man;
I live to help you all I can.

My Miracle

I call into the darkness,
        but I hear no reply.
        You're not close, not near.
I wander around clumsily,
        but I can't find you.
        You're lost to me, I fear.
I spoke to you in the womb,
        and you responded to me.
        You knew me even then.
I was there when you first breathed,
        tears of joy on my face.
        I can't believe how long it's been.
You've walked with me in my heart,
        since before you were born.
        I couldn't wait to meet you.
You walked with me in this earth
        for two years before we parted.
        O God - my heart is blue.
There will come another day,
        when I can nurture you once more.
        I'll do for you all I can.
Pay attention my young son,
        as I teach you all about life.
        I'll make sure you grow to be a good man.
There is much you must learn,
        to be a successful man.
        I want you to surpass your fathers.
You must have a strong will,
        and good self-discipline.
        So you can handle the world's bothers.

You're more important to me
      than I am to myself.
      I need you close to my heart.
If ever I had to face
      a future without you-
      My whole world would fall apart.
You are the main reason
      the blood pumps through my veins.
      I live for you, my son.
But, without doubt or hesitation,
      I'd lay down my life for yours.
      I'd die for you, my son.
I love you so much,
      I can't put it into words.
      You make me feel joy abounding.
Just to watch you live and grow
      overwhelms my soul with bliss.
      The miracle of you is astounding.
I need you in my life-
      I need to care for you again.
      You mean the world to me, my son.
I want to laugh and play with you,
      Get you out of bed every morning-
      Do things fun, and things not fun.
You need me there for you,
      To be your father you can look up to.
      I see it in your eyes.
Our time will someday come,
      you and me together again.
      Its written in God's skies.

A Child's Nightly Prayer (For Paul)

Dear God please protect my heart
Like You did from the very start.
Lord please watch over my soul.
When I wake up, please make me whole.

Momma

The phrase down and out can almost describe me –
    I've been down many times, but never out.
Wherever I may be, She always finds me.
    She's always there for me without a doubt.
My life has had successes and failures –
    Many times I've given up on myself.
But She's always believed that I'll someday succeed.
    Her faith in me is forever my real wealth.
I could go on about the things She has done.
    She's helped me many times throughout my life.
I have failed some pursuits, and let myself down.
    She's lessened my pain, suffering, and strife.
This woman of whom I speak gave birth to me.
    Without Her strength, I may have never breathed.
She suffered a great loss while I was still in the womb.
    She says I gave Her strength, made Her pain
        ease.
Her loss and my loss was the loss of my Father.
    He died before my eyes ever opened.
She suffered a Sunset, but I was a new day.
    Anticipation filled Her sails with new wind.
She's always told me that I bring Her good fortune,
    That I'm His memory in many ways.
I must live life to Her high expectations,
    Honoring Him, in Her eyes, all my days.

Love: Found, Lost, and Otherwise

Not Love

I could have loved you.
We could not let that happen,
But I could have loved you.
  The way you looked at me,
  The way I looked at you;
  There was something there.
    The way your touch felt,
    The way mine felt to you;
    There was something there.
I could have loved you,
If only we could let that happen.
A different place.
    A different time.
        Different circumstances.
            Maybe.
Maybe not just two ships passing,
  By way,
    Of that old cliché;
But something real.
Not just wasting time,
  Or burning time,
    Or losing time
        (Like those with limited time),
Like us.
We had no chance, no future,
But my heart didn't know that.
I told my heart to back off.
But that didn't matter
To a heart that was hooked
        On you.

I told my mind to straighten up,
But it was too busy swimming
In a pool filled with thoughts
        Of you.
Yeah, it's a good thing I didn't fall in love with you,
    Since we couldn't let that happen.
Love for us would have meant only pain,
Because we could never truly be together;
    At least not long enough.
As if any length of time
    Is long enough
        For two hearts in love.
I know that you can be happier without me,
    And that brings joy
        To a sorrowful heart,
            One that misses you already.
Your well being,
        To me,
Is more important than my own;
But I did not fall in love
(Because we could not let that happen),
        Or did I?

The First Time

He ran his eyes and his fingers (gently)
across the lines and contours of her outstretched form.
He lightly and softly caressed every inch of exposed,
delicate skin, so soft and smooth, so warm.

She yielded to his touch, and released
in his grasp, surrendering to his essence, which she felt
        through his hands.
The touch was hot like fire and electrifying, with a
        mystical sense of pleasure;
this touch, so dominant in her heart and mind, was
        unmistakably her man's.

They were lovers for the first time, touching, rubbing,
no longer speaking with words, but with whole bodies;
        they were making love.
It felt so thorough, so complete, each totally knowing the
        other;
their thoughts and feelings interlaced, this had to be a
        gift from above.

They felt as one now, their movements and undulations
        in unison;
he wanted more of her, and she of him, their appetites
        growing ever stronger.
When they finally returned from the world that they
        alone shared, they were exhausted, fatigued; now
        was the time to embrace and kiss, only changing
        the focus of their hunger.

For they still hungered one for another, for the touch,
    the scent,
even the taste of the love which they both felt.
Their hearts pounded, not from exhaustion, but from
    excitement,
exhilaration, for as one, in an inferno of desire, they
    knew they'd forever melt.

Was this love? Neither of them knew,
for their time together was short and sweet, the briefest
    of brief.
All that they could do was hold to one another
and prepare for the coming pain and grief.

Their love was doomed from the start,
no hope for a lasting affair.
But they wanted to chase forever,
even though true love is a thing most rare.

In the end they had to live for the now,
because their future was all but sure.
Soon they will have loved and lost,
but their love, though short-lived, is blessedly pure.

Angel Cries

My Angel cries
    when she talks to me.
Protecting my heart
    is pure futility.
I leave my feelings open,
    and keep getting hurt.
It seems that after once or twice,
    I'd be more alert.
But I continue to trust
    and give Love more chances.
For everything in life,
    true Love enhances.
Which makes it worthwhile
    to a heart lonely and blue.
My soul takes a beating,
    while true joy I pursue.
And so my Angel cries,
    because most times I'm in pain.
She doesn't realize I have nothing,
    but everything to gain.

over

please dry your eyes
i slowly die
i hurt inside
and don't know why

we were good
did all we could
but now we must
do what we should

the 'us' is passed
it went too fast
because we couldn't
make us last

so part we must
with no more fuss
and say good-bye
to what was us

Excused

I was in Heaven once,
      But then I was asked to leave.
The relationship, that is.
It was Heaven,
      Spending my time with her,
      The days, the nights –
      Even weekends.
I thought it was love.
Was I right? Was I wrong?
That makes no difference –
      She didn't think so.

Don't Walk By

I thought you noticed me
As I walked by
More than once.
I did not come talk to you
As I walked by –
I'm such a dunce.
I thought you would reject me
As I walked by
'Cause I have no game.
I should have stopped and talked
As I walked by.
I feel such shame.
You looked too beautiful
As I walked by,
And made no advance.
Your looks easily convinced me
As I walked by –
I had no chance.
I wanted to say something
As I walked by
But my mind froze.
I didn't have the courage
As I walked by
My story goes.

When confronted with great beauty
As I walk by
I'm at a loss.
I lack the needed confidence
As I walk by
At great cost.
I shoulda woulda coulda
As I walk by –
Scared to speak.
I can't handle rejection
As I walk by –
This makes me weak.
I must be stronger,
As I walk by,
Than my low esteem.
I must overcome,
As I walk by –
And catch my dreams.
I must realize,
As I walk by,
It's now or never.
My consequence,
As I walk by,
Is loneliness forever.

Typical Chick

Typical woman
    Typical chick –
    I should never let my guard down.

Less than a second after I saw her face,
I knew I had to talk to her.
Such a strong attraction, I could not escape –
Her smile was an irresistible lure.
We talked. We danced. I could not believe my good luck,
This woman was beautiful inside and out.
I let my guard down; let my heart have new hope,
Before I knew what she was all about.
I should have known better than to trust –
I learned that lesson long ago.
No woman is worth a stirring in the heart,
At the first sign of feeling, its time to go.

Typical woman
    Typical chick –
    I should never let my guard down.

She let me know more about her,
Than she let anyone else know.
She took me to places in her soul,
Where nobody else could ever go.
She made me feel special, and wanted.
I thought she was really into me.
Too late, I realized that my guard was down;
I guess I'm still plagued by naiveté.
She suckered me in – I thought it was safe to feel.
I was mistaken, I read her wrong.

When she finally made her true self known,
It was too late – my feelings were strong.
     Never again

Typical woman
     Typical chick –
     I should never let my guard down.

I can't believe it – I opened up to her;
I let her see what makes me tick.
I made a mistake, put a little trust in her –
Let myself feel for a typical chick.
I should've known better, but now I've learned –
A typical chick deserves no trust.
All women are alike – they don't get my heart;
Far too many times, it's been crushed.

Typical woman
     Typical chick –
     I should never let my guard down.

Don't Want It Back

I used to have a forever heart.
But now the forever-ness is gone.
> It was taken from me,
> By others and myself.
> I don't know if I want it back.

I used to have hope for my future and love.
But the hope was chased away by my suffering.
> It allowed me to be used,
> And trampled upon.
> I don't know if I want hope back.

I used to have dreams of a happily wed future.
But they were derailed by the reality of awake.
> They retreated from reach,
> Before my waking mind could hold them.
> I don't know if I want dreams back.

I used to trust fate to make everything right.
But that's not the role fate played in my life.
> I wanted true love,
> But I was detoured by fate.
> I don't know if I want trust back.

The One

Are you Her? Are you She? Are you the One?
    I thought I'd found you once or twice...
        But I was wrong.
    What I found was nothing nice,
        And they were wrong.
        For me.
My heart was optimistic in the past.
    I searched for love,
    Thought that I could find Her.
    The only person in this world for me.
I actually thought I could find true love and make it last.
    But life taught me better.
    She doesn't walk this earth.
    I learned that lesson quite painfully.
So from optimistic ashes, I arose.
    Been there, done that;
    Got the T-shirt and the scars,
    Pessimistic about love, thanks to life.
Now I think of myself as someone who knows.
    Love isn't worth the trouble,
    Love only brings pain.
    I'll grow old all alone with no wife.
Then you walked in.

Are you Her? Are you She? Are you the One?
    I feel hope where there was none.
    I have a smile where there wasn't one.
    My world doesn't weigh a ton.
    Dreary days have become fun.
Since you walked in.

Are you Her? Are you She? Are you the One?
  A new development in my heart –
    I feel hope where hope had died.
    Now my heart wants to be my guide,
    But my mind thinks joy and pain will
     collide.
  From this truth I cannot hide,
  I want to set my fears aside,
  And maybe open my heart wide –
    But would you tear it apart?
My mind's adrift with thoughts of you –
  You've touched my heart with yours.
My heart was locked to everyone –
  But you're opening the doors.
I knew I'd never love again,
  I'm no longer sure of this.
I've had to rethink my life's intent –
  My lonely heart insists.
Because you walked in.

Are you Her? Are you She? Are you the One?
  I don't know why I let hope in.
    You and me can never be.
  Our paths crossed at the wrong point in life,
    I'm sure that you agree.
  You may be She. You may be Her.
    The One who's meant to match my soul.
  But the time is wrong for us to love,
    So I remain out in the cold.

Are you Her? Are you She? Are you the One?

Hope Left?

There is a woman of my dreams,
    My very own Ms. Right.
The one made for me,
    Meant for me –
    My perfect match.
I know she lives for me,
    Though I haven't seen her.
I know she walks this earth,
    Though I'll never see her.
Evaded by happiness,
    I'm not to find true love;
    At least not embodied by her.
Everyone has a soul-mate –
    That potential partner for life.
    Right?
Even me – I have a soul-mate;
    I'm cursed to search, and never find her.
I can find Ms. Wrong without even trying,
    I've done so many times.
Occasionally, I thought I'd found the right one;
    The results were torturous to my soul.
I don't know why I've kept trying all these years;
    I'll never find her, she'll never find me.
    I've probably barely missed her many times –
        She walks in as I walk out,
        Or I enter as she leaves –
            The store
            The market
            Library
            Maybe everywhere I've been.

My search feels hopeless, senseless, self-punitive,
     But I can't quit, because I don't do that.
        Am I a glutton for pain and discontent?
        Or do I actually have hope left?
        (I thought it had left.)
Whatever the reason, my quest goes on.
     I know she's out there, so I can't give up...
     Even though I'll never find her.

Used

Cry me a river, buy me a liver;
    You drove me to drink.
Let you in my heart, you ripped it apart;
    It's dead and starting to stink.
I did all for you, 'cause I loved you, Boo;
    I only see shades of black.
All the pain I accrued is making me brood;
    I want all my effort back.
You made me blind, you softened my mind;
    Never again, I vow.
My hope is gone, I'll live life alone;
    Repeat I can not allow.
I don't know why, I believed your lie;
    You said you loved me.
Now that I'm burned, the lesson I've learned:
    Don't forgive hastily.

Hurtful

Aside I've been tossed.
My dejection is born of rejection.
I'm at a loss.
My outlook is bleak.
  I opened my heart.
  I didn't realize this would be my demise.
  It was such a good start.
  Her love was unique.
She convinced me to let myself feel her love,
  That I needed to open up.
She told me it was safe to hope for true love‐
  She didn't say where my hope would end up.
I opened my soul to her‐
  I let love out and in.
It was she who held back, rejecting my love.
  Realization was a telephone pole to my chin.

Morbid Description · Love Lost

I feel my heart crumbling within my sullen chest
   Into putrid chunks of rotting flesh.
Falling, falling into the pit of my stomach low-
   Nourishment, causing the dark side of me to grow.
The me that scares me,
   That I can never let out.
My thoughts are unnerving
   When that side of me shouts.
All the bad things from life-
   The negatives I experience,
Collect in a pit deep inside my soul,
   And keep that side of me in existence.
Love is more powerful than hate.
   Gone bad, it's far more destructive.
When love goes bad, it can mutilate a good heart.
   It can take away a man's will to give.
All semblance of kindness can be squeezed from a heart,
   A heart used and abused by hope and love.
Pain and agony, strife, a crushing destruction,
   May merely be testing what I'm made of.
If I fail, the dark side of me wins-
   In my heart, mind, and soul, it gains dominance.
I can't beat love gone bad; I know I can't win-
   I don't dwell on this unlikely occurrence.

Champion Heart

Could it be dawn already?
>Might the sun be rising
>For a heart, lost in the dark,
>Eclipsed by unhappiness?

I feel no joy,
But it's a start.
Rejection pains me still,
But it's a start.
I'll spring back completely -
My Champion Heart.
Soon my wounds will heal -
My Champion Heart.
At first I let it bother me,
Being used emotionally.
Then I concluded, no one's worth it -
The wreck of a sentimental me.
I can be strong all alone -
I've been there before.
I don't need entanglements of the heart,
Or should I call it Love's War?
Believe it or not, I'm still open to new love,
But I'll remain cautious and wary with my affection.
I'm not thoroughly bitter, though I'm slow to trust -
I'm not eager to add to my heart's war-wound collection.
But things are looking up -
>The hurt from before is gone,
>The door to joy slamming shut,
>The dread of loneliness from alone.

Yes, things are looking up ·
I'm discovering my true strength.
My Champion Heart will ever win,
Though, to the contrary, some go to great lengths.

Sensual

Tenderness.
Intimate silence.
Two heartbeats yearning for one another.
Warmth.
Gentle Passion.
A feather light touch on smooth, soft skin.
Together.
Holding Closely.
Arms and legs intertwined, no need to move.
Her head rests upon my chest,
     Where it belongs, where it should be,
     So light and peaceful that it calms my soul.
Her heart beats softly against my stomach,
     Its gentle rhythm nurtures more than food.
I listen as she breathes in the darkness,
     A sweet lullaby which lures me into a dream-like
         state.
Her touch is like warm, flowing water,
Pure pleasure to my thick, toughened skin,
Very soft and gentle, yet bold,
Because she knows she is where she belongs.
     I feel joy in the trust that she shows,
     With her complete surrender into me,
     She knows safety exists within my embrace,
     The very thought of this warming me to the core.
I caress her face and arms and back.
     I enjoy it.
I run my fingers through her hair.
     It soothes me.

I like to give and get a gentle touch,
While laying in the darkness.
That gentle warmth, the scent, the taste,
Are what a man truly wants from a woman.

Me

Soldier

I want to go home,
But I can't.
> Someone has to be here.

I want to duck and run,
But I can't.
> Not everyone can move through fear.

I need to take a rest,
But I can't.
> Sometimes you have to drive on.

I fear isolation,
But I can't.
> At times I must work alone.

I want to show emotion,
But I can't.
> A soft heart makes my job hard.

I want to relax,
But I can't.
> I must constantly be on guard.

I want to feel sorrow,
But I can't.
> This job is already tough.

I want to do more,
But I can't.
> Already, I'm fatigued enough.

I want to avoid hardship,
But I can't.
> Not everyone can handle it, as I.

I want to be lazy,
But I can't.
> Those challenges of life, I must try.

I want to be a soldier,
And I can.
     Not everyone is able.
I need to be proud of my work,
And I can.
     Soldier is a pretty good label.
I want to protect the innocent,
And I can.
     That makes everything worthwhile.
I want to make the world better,
And I can.
     That's why I go the extra mile.

Easy Day

It's a good day,
A lazy day...

I sit on my porch,
And watch the world around me.
I feel the warmth from my old dog,
Who's keeping me company.
I watch the sun rise at dawn,
I'm still sitting when it sets.
I hear reminisces of the past
From two old war vets.
I see Miss Mary Magdalene
Hangin' up her clothes.
Where she gets her strength,
God only knows.
I hear the baby cryin';
He don't wanna sleep upstairs.
I can't say I blame him –
It's way too hot up there.
I like it right here on my porch,
It's just the place for me.
And my big ole' chair is broken in –
It's nice and soft and cozy.
I take a glance down the street,
And see a few kids playin'.
And then came the preacher walkin' by –
He took the day off from prayin'.
Yeah, it's a good day to relax,
And take things nice and slow;
Doze off and wake up –
That's how days like this go.

My mood's easy and laid back,
I don't have a care in the world.
Where good days are concerned,
This one is a pearl.

My Own Eyes

When I'm alone, I'm really not,
　There's always a reflection around.
The only way to evade my own gaze
　Is to stare, unseeing, at the ground.
My own eyes look right through me⁻
　They see straight to the core.
They know all that I am, good and bad,
　Everything · no less, no more.
In my reflection, those eyes stare back harshly;
　Unyielding; Cold, calculated thought.
I try to hide from my own eyes, when I'm ashamed,
　But those efforts are all for naught.
Sometimes I fear what's in my eyes ·
　Am I a good or bad man?
As they bore into my soul, can those eyes behold
　If I've done all the good that I can?
I think my own eyes feel disappointment,
　When they peer deep into my soul.
I think they can see that despite my best efforts,
　At my center is a bleak hole.
There are too many things that I haven't done right;
　I've wasted my time here on earth.
When I see this reflected in my own eyes,
　I must question my self-worth.

Not Broken

I have a mind of my own –
Can't this world see?
I just want equal footing –
Why can't that be?
I bother no one –
Why bother me?
Harassed in my home –
This country's free?
Brought here in chains –
Our destiny?
Beaten and hanged –
For trying to flee?
Not allowed to learn –
By State decree?
Taught not to yearn –
Successfully?
Lived with scorn and hate –
What's wrong with me?
I can never be great –
Why limit me?
I won't be held down –
This I decree.
I'll reach for the stars –
Passionately.
One day I'll break through –
I see clearly.
I do all for my Son –
Not just for me.

Alone

Half moon. Dark night.
        All alone.
No companion for companionship,
        I'm lonely-prone.
I blow little smoke rings
        Into the humid night.
They share their lives with me –
        Until they drift out of sight.
I've been alone before,
        But not lonely then.
It's when companionship is over
        That loneliness sets in.
My life's a conundrum –
        What can a man do?
I want a companion in my life –
        But I want to be alone, too.
Relationships in my life
        Have turned me from love.
They've scarred me in ways
        I'd before not thought of.
This is why I want
        To let the loneliness be.
When I'm all alone,
        I'm free to be me.
But at the very same time,
        I want a woman in my world.
Someone to cherish –
        My very own precious pearl.
What's a man to do
        With a conflicting heart?

Which way should I go
        With this – a new start?
Should I try love again?
        Take another chance?
Is it possible for me
        To win in romance?
Or make the lonely road mine?
        A peaceful destiny...
A desolate heart –
        But no one to alter me.
My dilemma is manifest
        In my socio-condition.
I try to relate, but I fail
        Due to my "be-alone" mission.
I want to fill my heart's needs,
        But that can never be done.
I relish this new freedom,
        But this loneliness ways a ton.

Alone II

Same kind of night,
    But where's the moon?
A few stars in the sky,
    But there's no moon.
I scan the dark sky
    For my loneliness companion.
I ask the stars why
    I can't depend on this companion.
I have not a soul to talk to –
    All alone once again.
Just a cigar to smoke through –
    My only loneliness bane.
I'm not yet used to being lonely –
    My heart's still teaching me how to cope.
Before, it would not have paid to bet
    That alone-ness would make me lose such hope.

Iron Must Yield

The War rages on
Battle after battle
Blood, sweat, and tears
With no remorse at all.

Flesh and bone scream
Under the crushing weight
Iron must yield
Life itself is at stake.

Pain is abundant
It tries to drain the life from me
That will never happen
It feeds my intensity.

Agony tests my soul
Tries to blur my mind
My Warrior Spirit is stronger
I left fear and weakness behind.

LaVergne, TN USA
23 February 2011

217390LV00002B/39/P